100%
UNOFFICIAL
FOOTBALL
IDOLS

Your guide to France's
PACY PRODIGY

MBAPPÉ

DEAN

First published in Great Britain in 2021 by Dean,
part of Farshore.

An imprint of HarperCollins*Publishers*
1 London Bridge Street, London SE1 9GF
www.farshore.co.uk

HarperCollins*Publishers*
1st Floor, Watermarque Building, Ringsend Road
Dublin 4, Ireland

Written by Kevin Pettman
Edited by Craig Jelley
Designed by Grant Kempster and Jessica Coomber

This book is an original creation by Farshore

This unofficial guide is in no way connected to or sponsored by Kylian Mbappé

100% Unofficial Football Idols: Mbappé © Farshore 2021

ISBN 978 0 7555 0205 9
Printed in Italy
1

A CIP catalogue record for this title is available from the British Library.

Farshore takes its responsibility to the planet and its inhabitants very seriously.
We aim to use papers from well-managed forests run by responsible suppliers.

100% UNOFFICIAL

FOOTBALL

IDOLS

Your guide to France's
PACY PRODIGY

MBAPPÉ

CONTENTS

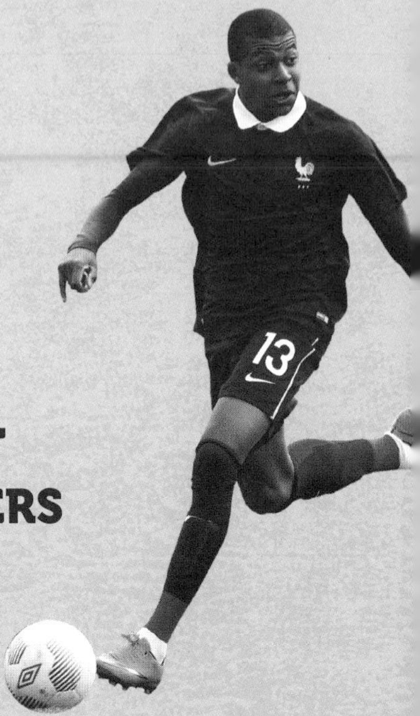

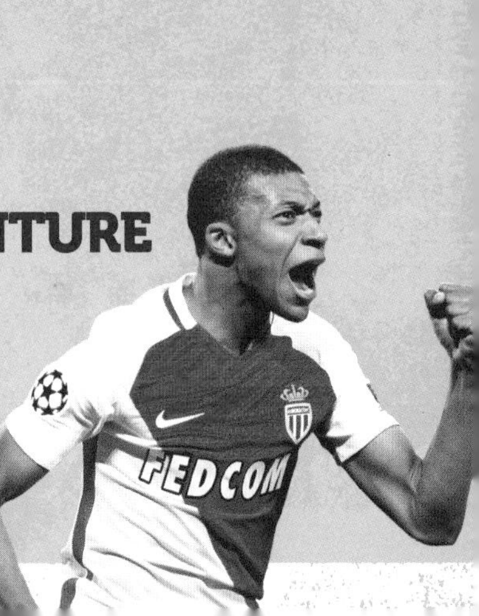
FEDCOM

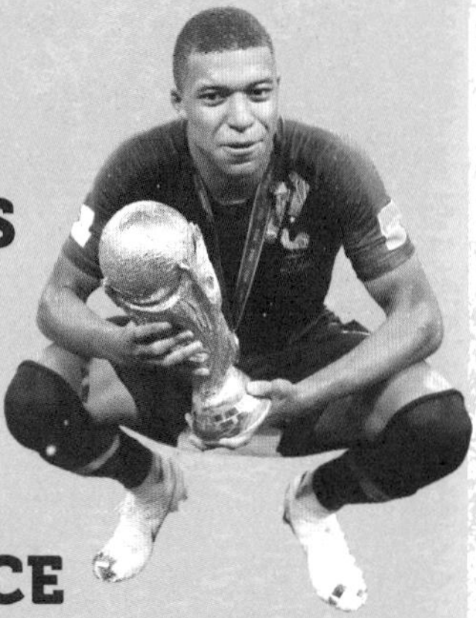

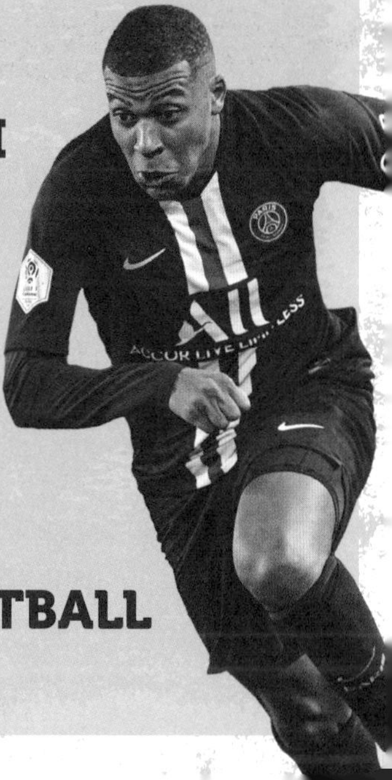
ALL
ACCOR LIVE LIMITLESS

MEET MBAPPÉ

KYLIAN MBAPPÉ

Born: 20 December, 1998

Birthplace: Paris

Country: France

Club: Paris Saint-Germain (PSG)
Previous clubs: Monaco, AS Bondy (Youth)

Position: Forward

Preferred foot: Right

With awesome goals, slick skills and millions of fans, Kylian Mbappé is one of the hottest players in the world! The speedy star rocketed into the record books as a talented teenager, becoming a World Cup and Champions League hero in his first few seasons as a pro. He's already a legend and ranks with the game's greats like Messi and Ronaldo!

By the age of 20, Mbappé had already smashed over 100 career goals, won multiple titles and blasted France to glory. His mega move to PSG made him the most expensive teenager of all time. Kylian's goal threat delivers trophies for him and his team – he's a nightmare for defenders to stop!

Mbappé's rapid rise has taken him on a magical journey on and off the pitch. In this *Football Idols* book, you'll discover all you need to know about him, from his first footy-steps as a kid to his greatest goals and glories. It's time to kick off Kylian's adventure!

KYLIAN THE KID

Even as a small boy growing up in Paris, Mbappé wanted to be a footy hero

Ever since he was a young lad, Kylian Mbappé had a passion for football. He was kicking a ball even as a toddler and was always encouraged by his footy-mad dad. Kylian was born in Bondy, a suburb just a few miles north of Paris. His earliest memories are of AS Bondy, his childhood club, where dad Wilfried worked as a youth team coach. With an upbringing like this, you could say he was born to be a footballer!

FOOTY FACT

In Mbappé's hometown of Bondy, this cool street art on the side of a tower block shows him dreaming of football glory with France!

It was clear Mbappé was going to become a professional footballer. Watching his heroes, such as Zinedine Zidane and Cristiano Ronaldo, perform their magic on TV gave him the dream to do exactly the same one day.

Bondy

PARIS

When he was not at the club's pitches or having kickabouts with friends near his home, Kylian liked to bring his skills inside. One of his first coaches at AS Bondy remembers him turning the family lounge into a pitch, using the sofa as a goal. Fortunately for Kylian, he never broke anything in the house!

BONDY BOY

"Kylian could do much more than the other children. His dribbling was already fantastic and he was much faster than the others."
Antonio Riccardi, AS Bondy coach, suggesting that Kylian was a star from a very early age. He's still young and will still get better too!

He's a global superstar now, but Kylian will never forget where his football skills shone as a boy. AS Bondy, his first club, remains with him forever. He started playing with them aged five, but club officials remember that even when he was two, Kylian would walk around with a ball and watch the teams and listen to the coaches!

His dad, Wilfried, had trained youth teams for many years at AS Bondy and Kylian inherited his football brain. Coached by his father and others at the club, his natural talent for scoring goals and assisting was obvious. He was soon playing with older age groups, to make sure he was challenged and continued to improve. Awareness of his talent began to spread around the country and beyond, and many scouts came to watch him play at Bondy.

Zidane, Michel Platini and Thierry Henry are the most exciting French footballers of the last 40 years, and they all achieved greatness for club and country. The talk was that this brilliant Bondy boy could match, or even eclipse, them all.

FOOTY

The Mbappés are a very sporty bunch and the brothers make a top attacking trio!

WILFRIED

You've already discovered that his dad has been involved with football for most of his life. He was born in Cameroon and cheered as the country stormed the 1990 World Cup.

FAYZA

When Wilfried settled in France, he met Fayza, his future wife. It's no surprise their children would also become athletes. Fayza was a top player in the popular sport of handball.

FAMILY

JIRES

If Kylian wanted another person to look up to, his adopted older sibling was already making progress as a pro. Jires Kembo Ekoko, who is 11 years older than Kylian, also starred for AS Bondy and went on to play as a forward for Rennes in Ligue 1, as well as the France Under-21 team.

ETHAN

To complete the football family tree, Kylian has a younger bro who is ripping it up for the PSG youth teams! Watch out for Ethan Mbappé carrying on the family's footballing dynasty in the future.

FOOTY FACT

Mbappé's goal celebration, when he stands with arms crossed, is something his little brother does when playing FIFA on the PlayStation!

SOCCER SCHOOL

Mbappé starred at the special Clairefontaine football academy

South-west of Paris, there's a very famous football academy, Clairefontaine which offers coaching to impressive, young footballers from northern France. Once selected, kids from the age of 12 to 15 get special coaching and the opportunity to develop into the country's finest young talent.

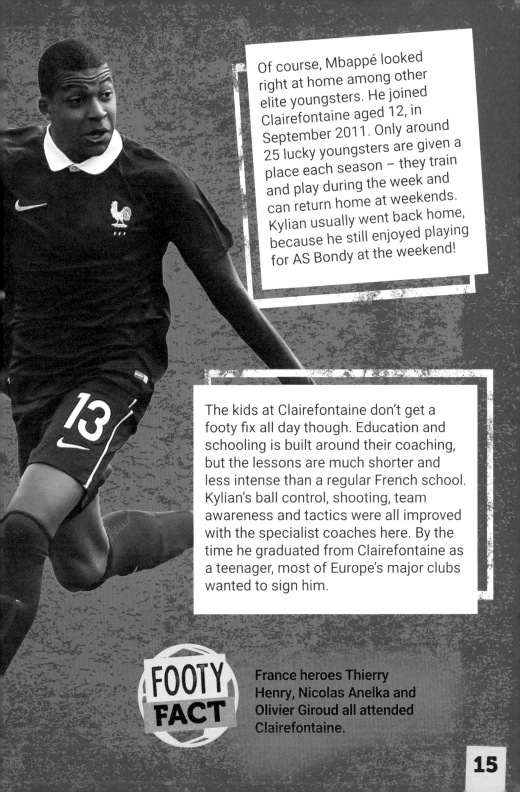

Of course, Mbappé looked right at home among other elite youngsters. He joined Clairefontaine aged 12, in September 2011. Only around 25 lucky youngsters are given a place each season – they train and play during the week and can return home at weekends. Kylian usually went back home, because he still enjoyed playing for AS Bondy at the weekend!

The kids at Clairefontaine don't get a footy fix all day though. Education and schooling is built around their coaching, but the lessons are much shorter and less intense than a regular French school. Kylian's ball control, shooting, team awareness and tactics were all improved with the specialist coaches here. By the time he graduated from Clairefontaine as a teenager, most of Europe's major clubs wanted to sign him.

FAVE FOOTBALLERS

As a young footy player, Mbappé worshipped these world-class stars

Kylian had posters of the Portuguese superstar all over his bedroom! He adored Ronaldo when he became a goalscoring machine at Real Madrid, and even before when he rocked at Man United. Kylian loved to copy Ronaldo's moves.

CRISTIANO RONALDO

Before Cristiano came along, legendary Brazil forward Ronaldo was the ultimate striker! Kylian marvelled at how Ronaldo could power past defenders and dribble and trick his way to scoring incredible goals. Like Kylian, Ronaldo also starred in World Cup finals.

RONALDO

ZINEDINE ZIDANE

Although Zidane was a midfield maestro and not a forward like Mbappé, he still thought of the France and Real Madrid hero as an incredible player. He won the World Cup and Champions League in a glittering career but Mbappé was only seven when Zidane retired, so he didn't see him play that much!

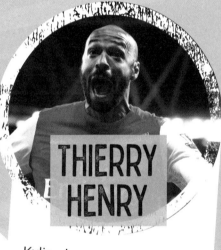

THIERRY HENRY

Kylian has often been compared to the iconic France and Arsenal striker, who stopped playing in 2014. Henry had electric pace, excellent dribbling ability and a smart head on his shoulders too. Kylian and Henry both began their careers with Monaco too.

CLUB CALL-UP

The big boys came calling for the talented superkid

As he left Clairefontaine in the summer of 2013, Kylian had his pick of big clubs to begin his professional career at. Actually, even before then he had already spent time at Chelsea and Real Madrid!

Aged 11, he and his family enjoyed a week in London with Chelsea. He was given a Chelsea shirt with his name on the back and met the manager, Carlo Ancelotti. Mbappé impressed playing in a youth game for Chelsea, alongside future Blues striker Tammy Abraham, but he wasn't interested in joining the Premier League club.

It was the same story at Real Madrid a few years later. The Mbappé family loved their tour of the La Liga giants, chatting with the players and receiving a special shirt, but still Kylian wasn't keen to move to Spain.

The list of other epic clubs desperate to sign him included Arsenal, Bayern Munich, Borussia Dortmund, Juventus and Manchester City. However, much to the football world's surprise, he chose to stay in France. His supersonic rise as a Ligue 1 legend was about to take off!

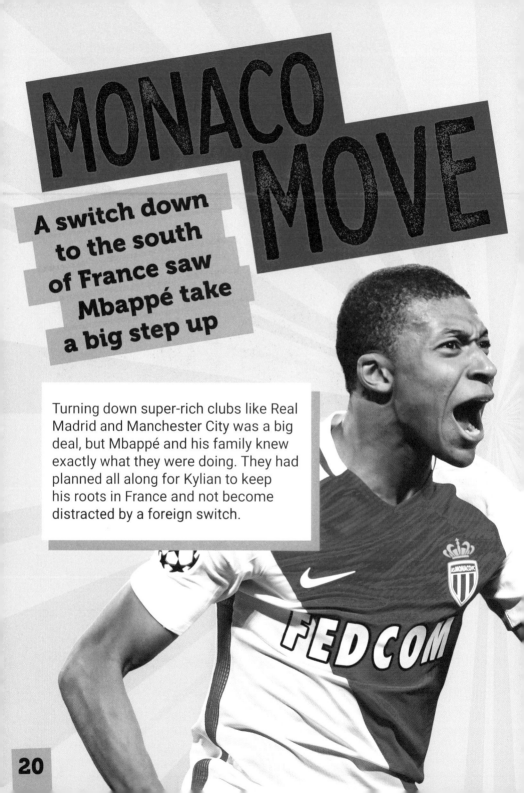

MONACO MOVE

A switch down to the south of France saw Mbappé take a big step up

Turning down super-rich clubs like Real Madrid and Manchester City was a big deal, but Mbappé and his family knew exactly what they were doing. They had planned all along for Kylian to keep his roots in France and not become distracted by a foreign switch.

Joining an ambitious Monaco team was a smart decision. He was only 14, but Monaco had just returned to Ligue 1 and were happy to promote their young players and mix them with some big-money signings.

Rather than competing with other high-class international teenagers in the Premier League or La Liga, Kylian got the attention he needed at Monaco. The coaches there allowed him to develop his game, with the only pressure being his own desire to reach the first team. It wouldn't be long before his chance would come to show how good he was at Monaco.

"I have had a career plan since my youngest age. I know what I want to do, where I want to go." – Kylian's stratospheric rise is a result of a solid plan. He knew he'd become a world-beating striker!

Seeing a teenage Anthony Martial, only three years older than Mbappé, getting goals for Monaco assured him that he could do the same. After Martial made an expensive move to Manchester United in 2015, it was time for Kylian to become the next big thing in France.

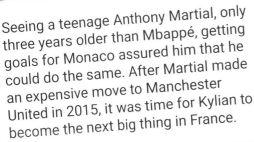

2015-2016 – MONACO

SEASON TO SHINE

Check out Mbappé's breakthrough season as he became one of France's most feared teenagers

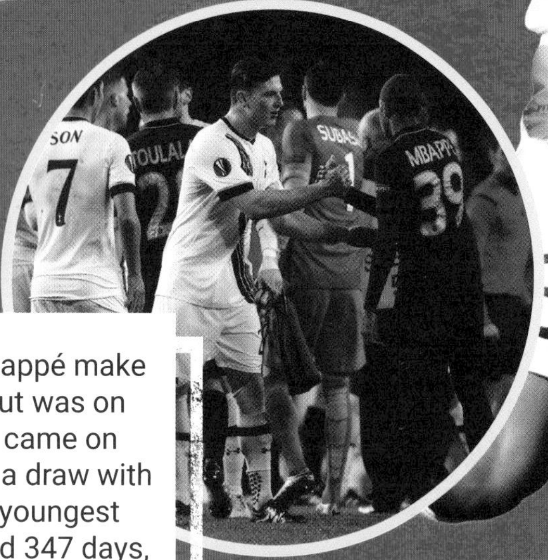
SON
7

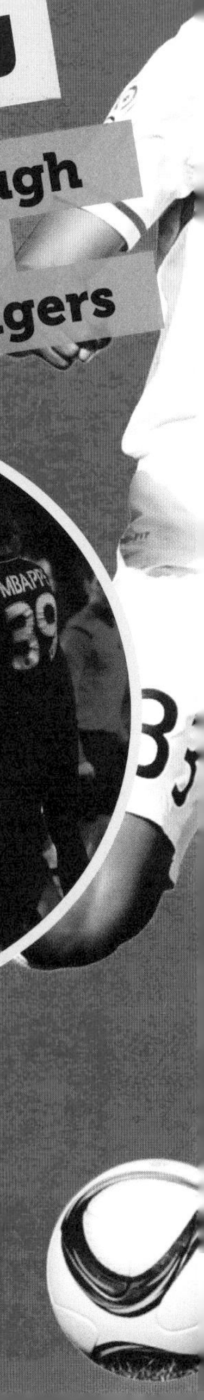

The 2015-16 season saw Mbappé make his mark at Monaco. His debut was on 2nd December 2015, when he came on as an 88th-minute sub during a draw with Caen. It made him the club's youngest ever player, aged 16 years and 347 days, breaking the record set by Thierry Henry. A week later, he played nearly the whole second half of a Europa League game at Tottenham, assisting their only goal. At this point he still didn't have a pro deal!

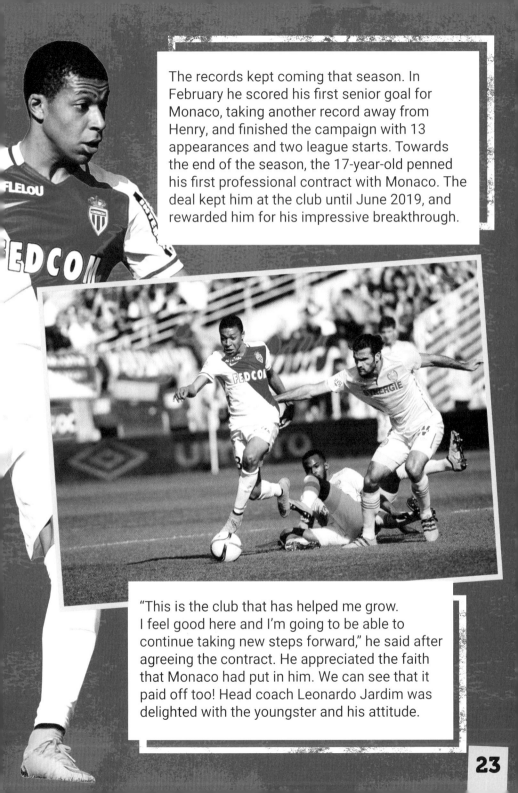

The records kept coming that season. In February he scored his first senior goal for Monaco, taking another record away from Henry, and finished the campaign with 13 appearances and two league starts. Towards the end of the season, the 17-year-old penned his first professional contract with Monaco. The deal kept him at the club until June 2019, and rewarded him for his impressive breakthrough.

"This is the club that has helped me grow. I feel good here and I'm going to be able to continue taking new steps forward," he said after agreeing the contract. He appreciated the faith that Monaco had put in him. We can see that it paid off too! Head coach Leonardo Jardim was delighted with the youngster and his attitude.

TEENAGE TRIUMPH

Mbappé's first trophy with Monaco arrived after a stunning final show

Even though he was now a first-team star, Kylian still led the Monaco Under-19 team to a memorable trophy in May 2016. The French Youth Cup, called the Gambardella Cup, is a chance for teenage stars to showcase their skills. Monaco had lifted the trophy three times in the past, but hadn't appeared in the final since 2011.

With Mbappé in their attack, Monaco easily outsmarted Lens in the cup final at the Stade de France in Paris. It was his first trophy with the club and he scored two awesome goals. His first strike saw him sprint clear from the centre circle and beat the keeper with an accurate low shot, followed by a powerful angled drive inside the box after beating two defenders.

His performance once again proved he was a big player for big occasions. Looking a class above the players around him, even though they were all a similar age to him, it was clear the 17-year-old was ready for a full campaign spearheading Monaco's first team. This victory was the start of an epic year of football for him.

EURO STAR

As France's most thrilling youngster, he guided them to a great European trophy

Following his Gambardella Cup heroics, Mbappé joined the France squad in July 2016, to take part in the UEFA Under-19 European Championship. After securing his first trophy with Monaco, he was hoping to win another with his national teammates.

Despite losing their opening game to England, the French hit back to reach the semi-finals with wins over Croatia and the Netherlands. Mbappé bagged three goals in the first three games and added two more in the 3-1 semi-final win against Portugal. This set up a final with Italy, but Mbappé and his mates were too strong and produced a record 4-0 win.

Reflecting on the win, Mbappé was very pleased with his display. "It was my first international competition. It was very important for me because I was representing my country, which is priceless," he said. He was proud of himself, but he also made a whole nation proud as well!

Manchester City offered Monaco £36 million for Mbappé after the Under-19 Championships, but the club said no.

MONACO MAGIC

The title belonged to Monaco in 2017, thanks to the brilliance of Mbappé in his first full season as a professional

One of Monaco's most memorable recent seasons came in 2016-17. After finishing third the season before, and a massive 31 points behind champions PSG, they turned on the style to win their first Ligue 1 title in 17 years.

FOOTY FACT

Mbappé was named Ligue 1 Young Player of the Year in 2017 and was also part of the official Team of the Year.

Mbappé was injured in the opening game of the season and endured a slow start. When he regained fitness and netted his first goal in late October, he never looked back. His first hat-trick came in a cup game in December, followed by his first league hat-trick in a 5-0 thrashing of Metz helping Monaco keep up with PSG.

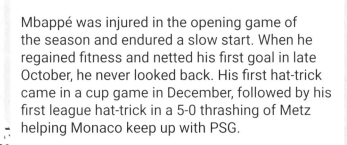

With support from stars such as Bernardo Silva, Radamel Falcao and Fabinho, 18-year-old Mbappé became a lethal forward. In the second half of the season he scored 12 goals and a further eight assists in the league. He scored in the title-clinching 2-0 win over St. Etienne as the teenager took Monaco to an incredible league crown. But his incredible campaign didn't end there – Monaco were still going toe-to-toe with Europe's best in the Champions League ...

EUROPEAN ADVENTURE

Could the kid take on the best in the Champions League?

Of course he could!

As unforgettable as Monaco's Ligue 1 triumph was, their heroics in the Champions League were also off the charts. Nobody thought they'd progress from their group, which featured Tottenham, Bayer Leverkusen and CSKA Moscow, especially after two tricky qualifying rounds.

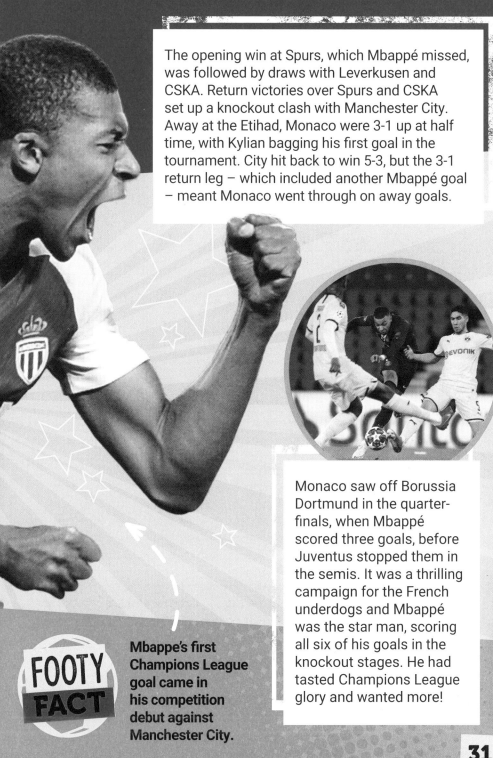

The opening win at Spurs, which Mbappé missed, was followed by draws with Leverkusen and CSKA. Return victories over Spurs and CSKA set up a knockout clash with Manchester City. Away at the Etihad, Monaco were 3-1 up at half time, with Kylian bagging his first goal in the tournament. City hit back to win 5-3, but the 3-1 return leg – which included another Mbappé goal – meant Monaco went through on away goals.

Monaco saw off Borussia Dortmund in the quarter-finals, when Mbappé scored three goals, before Juventus stopped them in the semis. It was a thrilling campaign for the French underdogs and Mbappé was the star man, scoring all six of his goals in the knockout stages. He had tasted Champions League glory and wanted more!

FOOTY FACT

Mbappe's first Champions League goal came in his competition debut against Manchester City.

PSG
PARTY!

In the hottest summer transfer ever, big-spending PSG brought Mbappé home

Having failed to sign him in the past, there was now no way that Europe's major clubs would pass up Mbappé in the summer of 2017. He had just won the league for Monaco and taken them to the Champions League semis – the kid was hot stuff!

"For any young person from the Paris region, it is often a dream to wear the red and blue jersey and experience the unique atmosphere of the Parc des Princes." Kylian knew that he had topped the heights he'd worked so hard to reach. And deservedly so!

Despite interest from Arsenal, Man United and Real Madrid, it was Paris Saint-Germain who did a huge deal to capture football's most exciting teenager. Mbappé was so happy to be staying in France and to begin playing at the Parc des Princes stadium, near where he grew up.

It was the second most expensive deal in history, costing PSG an incredible £165 million. The only player more costly was Neymar, who was also bought by PSG from Barcelona for £200 million just a few weeks before. What a dream team strikeforce in Paris!

It was an astonishing amount to pay for a teenager with just one full season in the game, but PSG had seen enough to know that Kylian would develop into one of the most exciting footballers France had ever seen.

7 SLICK

This is what makes Mbappé such a supreme performer on the pitch

1 SHOOTING

Mbappé has the power and the precision to shoot from anywhere on the pitch – long range outside the box, accurate close-up finishes and even free-kicks from difficult angles. He can fire off a snapshot in an instant.

3 DRIBBLING

Kylian can create a chance or shooting opportunity from nothing, just by using his dribbling skills to drive towards the opposition's goal. It's like the ball is glued to his boots!

2 CREATIVITY

As well as being a scoring sensation, Mbappé delivers bags of goal chances for his teammates. In his first 180 career games, he recorded an eye-catching 58 assists and coaches love a player that either scores or assists in virtually every game!

SKILLS

4 PACE

Whether or not he has the ball, Mbappé uses his speed to devastating effect. He's one of the quickest players around!

5 TRICKS

Mbappé has more magic than a wizard's wand! He's not just a showoff though. He uses his tricks to beat defenders and get his team attacking.

7 VERSATILITY

The youngster can play as a central striker, or on either wing in support of a target man. His willingness to adapt and change tactics or position during a game is invaluable.

6 LISTENING

Even as a teen, Kylian had the concentration and awareness to listen to his coaches and fellow pros and learn from them.

5 FAST

Hold on tight — these quick-fire Kylian stats will blow you away!

1 FAST FORWARD

Mbappé has been recorded reaching speeds of nearly 28 mph on the pitch. This puts him in the league of Olympic sprinters! His speed means he can leave defenders for dust, race into the penalty area and score or create stacks of goals. Mbappé's got a need for speed!

2 HELPING HAND

Mbappé is paid millions to play football and by the companies that sponsor him, but he's not a selfish person. He donated the money he received for playing at the World Cup — over £250,000 — to a children's sporting charity. What a nice guy!

FOOTY FACTS

3 FAN-TASTIC

Kylian loves playing football, and when he's not playing he wants to watch it on TV. "I watch all the games in all the leagues and I never get bored. I love it!" he says.

4 FIFA STAR

He became the global cover star for the EA Sports FIFA 21 video game. "Being on the cover of FIFA is a dream come true."

5 SEVEN HEAVEN

Mbappé says the number 7 shirt, which he now wears for PSG, is a famous shirt to have. "Seven is a legendary number, a lot of great players have worn it. I hope I'll do justice to this great number."

SAY WHAT?

Find out what some of football's most famous faces think about Mbappé

"When I watch him dribble, I can see what he's thinking. He uses his head when he plays and that, to me, is the most important thing for a player — he uses his brain."
Thierry Henry, France World Cup winner, sees Mbappé is as smart as he is talented. We think his brains take him to the next level.

"I don't want to give him too much praise, but he deserves it. What he's achieved at his age is outstanding."
Didier Deschamps, France coach, sees the talent in Kylian but hopes to keep him grounded. He'll get much more praise from us though ...

"To me, it's like he's 30 already. He's so mature and so rounded. It's a privilege for me to play with him."
Neymar, PSG teammate, recognises that Kylian's talent belies his years. He's going to be on another level when he is 30!

"I love him, to be honest. What a player he is and a nice lad as well, so he's a really good kid. What a player, what a player!"
Jurgen Klopp, Liverpool manager rates Kylian's personality as highly as his skills. Who doesn't love him?

"Mbappé is the future and the present. He's a fantastic player, very fast, and he will be the future."
Cristiano Ronaldo, Portugal captain, appreciates his talent. It won't be long before Mbappé is considered one of the greats like him.

LEAGUE LEADER

The striker enjoyed a brilliant year at PSG after his big move from Monaco

With the spotlight shining bright on Kylian Mbappé in his first season with PSG, he didn't disappoint and recorded another goal-packed, trophy-laden season. Forming a potent strikeforce alongside Neymar and Edinson Cavani, PSG were unstoppable in all three French domestic competitions.

Mbappé opened his account for PSG on his debut in a 5-1 thrashing of Metz with a classy right-footed goal. Neymar and Cavani also netted in the game as an omen of the trouble they would cause that season! The teenager finished the season with 21 goals in 46 appearances, including four in Europe as PSG reached the round of 16.

Kylian kept his assist rate high in his first season at the Parc des Princes. He assisted seven times in 28 Ligue 1 games, plus three in Europe and five in cup games. With the league title, French Cup and French League Cup in his trophy cabinet, no one thought his £165 million price tag was too high now!

FOOTY FACT

In 2018, Mbappé was named French Player of the Year and Ligue 1 Young Player of the Year (again).

FANTASTIQUE FRANCE

With the World Cup on the horizon, Mbappé answered the call to lead his country's attack

Mbappé's glory with Monaco and PSG was being closely watched by the coaches of the national team. Having starred for France at Under-17 and Under-19 level, scoring seven times in 13 youth games, he got his first call to the senior squad in March 2017. He made his debut against Luxembourg, aged only 18 years three months and five days, becoming France's youngest player in 62 years.

His first international goal came in August 2017, in a World Cup qualifying win against the Netherlands. He appeared 10 times for the national team in 2017, scoring once and making three assists as France booked their spot at the World Cup Finals.

Mbappé's selection for the France squad in the 2018 World Cup in Russia seemed assured as he continued to impress for PSG that season. What he wasn't expecting was to be given the famous no.10 shirt for the tournament. Previously worn by players like Zidane and Platini, it showed how much Les Bleus valued their prized striker on the eve of the World Cup.

FOOTY FACT

Mbappé was the first player born after France's World Cup final win in 1998 to be a part of the national team.

WORLD CUP WONDER

At Russia 2018, the world was ready to see him in action on the biggest stage

There was no doubt that he would play his part for France at the 2018 World Cup in Russia, but few expected him to take off so rapidly! His form leading into the competition was perfect, having scored in a USA friendly a week before the first game with Australia.

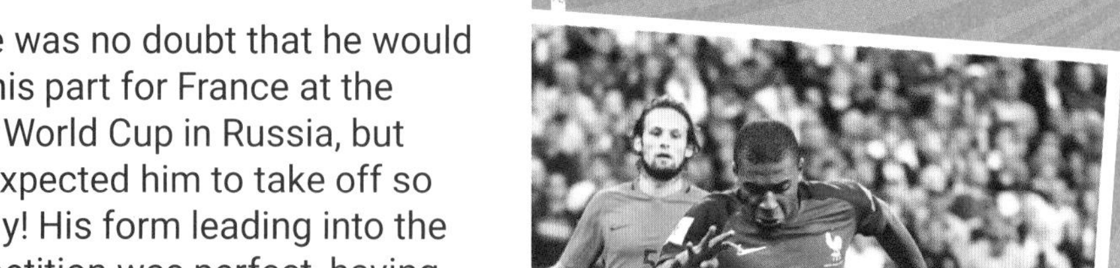

When Kylian started in France's opening win against Australia, he became the country's youngest ever World Cup player at 19 years and 178 days. Five days later, he started again and netted the only goal in a win over Peru that put Les Bleus into the next round.

It was in the knockout rounds when Mbappé really lit up the World Cup. Against Lionel Messi's Argentina, he scored a quick double that defeated the South Americans in a narrow 4-3 win. He worked hard as France battled to beat Uruguay in the quarter-final and in the semi-final with the Belgians, Mbappé looked awesome on the right side of a front three with Olivier Giroud and Antoine Griezmann. A 1-0 victory against Belgium set Mbappé on the road to the final.

WORLD

Six goals, refereeing controversy and a sparkling display from a red-hot teenager – the 2018 FIFA World Cup final had it all! Balanced at 2-1 at half-time, Mbappé also got on the scoresheet in the second half, adding the fourth goal in their 4-2 win against Croatia. Mbappé's cool finish, after taking two quick touches and blasting low outside the box, made him the first teenager to score in a final since Brazil's Pelé in 1958.

BEATER

Croatia pulled a goal back but it wasn't enough to beat Mbappé and his pals, and France won the World Cup for just the second time in history. Scenes of Mbappé celebrating the victory were seen by millions around the globe.

"To win a World Cup is something wonderful. We brought the country together."

Mbappé's skills and goals across all seven of France's games landed him the FIFA World Cup Best Young Player prize and a spot in the World Cup Dream Team. Not many players get the chance to appear in the final, let alone score and take the famous trophy home to their fans. Mbappé did exactly that in emphatic style.

PSG PALS

The most expensive double act in world footy are fearsome together and the best of friends in Paris

Fans wondered how two world-class strikers would get on together after their big-money transfers to PSG in 2017. Would they play like rivals? Would they disrupt the team? Not at all, because Mbappé and Neymar are pals on and off the pitch and the trophies they have won together already shows good value for their combined cost of £360 million!

"I really appreciate the relationship we have. He's like a big brother to me," Mbappé has said. "It's amazing to play with him." Of course, the whole footballing world can see what a dangerous attacking duo the pair are.

The stats for the strike pair are amazing. Together they netted over 150 times during their first three seasons in Paris, with the goals flowing in Ligue 1, the Champions League and French cups. Edinson Cavani formed a top trio with them until he left in 2020, with Argentina striker Mauro Icardi making an instant impact after he arrived in the 2019-20 season.

PSG GOALS SCORED

	2017-18	2018-19	2019-20
Mbappé	21	39	27
Neymar	28	23	19

LIKES AND LOVES

What's Mbappé like away from the pitch? Get up close and personal with him off the field

SOCIAL STAR
He has over 42 million followers on Instagram and around five million on Twitter. Kylian is not super flashy on social media, preferring to post about his friends and family rather than luxury cars and shopping. That said, his accounts show that he lives a super-cool lifestyle!

FASHION MAN

He's as smooth off the pitch as he is on it! Mbappé rocks it in relaxed sports gear, as well as bright jackets, baseball caps and classy suits. At a fashion show in China in July 2019, he even dressed up in a daring PSG-coloured dressing gown!

CHARITY WORK

'Inspired By KM' is a charity project he launched in 2020. It will help 98 youngsters aged nine to 16, from all social backgrounds, to develop and achieve their life goals. The four values that Kylian and the charity works on are to learn, understand, share and pass on.

SPORTS WATCH

He's a big football fan, but Mbappé also follows basketball, and in particular the NBA. When there have been NBA games in Paris, Mbappé and his mates love to hangout courtside! He's also been snapped watching tennis at the French Open and has spoken about wanting to be part of the French Olympic team and to win a gold medal in football!

TROPHY TIME

Following on from his World Cup victory, the 2018-19 season with PSG was another stunning show

Mbappé collected his third Ligue 1 medal in a row in 2019, and also picked up the league's Golden Boot award along the way, netting 33 times in only 29 appearances. That made him the youngest ever player to reach 30 goals in a single league season!

In total he registered 39 goals in 43 outings for PSG that season, also landing 17 assists. In an early 5-0 win over Lyon, he scored four goals for the first time and clocked his 50th PSG goal in that campaign as well, which he'd achieved in just 76 games. He also scored a hat-trick in a 9-0 crushing of Guingamp, which set a new record as PSG's biggest home victory.

His goals-per-game ratio rose astronomically, up to an average of 0.91 from 0.46 the season before. In 2018-19 he also won the prized Ligue 1 Player of the Year award for the first time. It had been won by three PSG greats in the previous three years – Neymar, Cavani and Zlatan Ibrahimovic.

GREATER THAN MESSI AND RONALDO?

The awards, goals and stats suggest Mbappé may be more lethal than these greats!

Fans can argue for hours about who is the best ever player. The case for Kylian being better than Lionel Messi or Cristiano Ronaldo is a strong one! He was only 18 years and 120 days old when he scored his fifth Champions League goal for Monaco, with Messi scoring only once in his first five European games at Barcelona. He reached ten Champions League goals at a record age of 18 years and 350 days.

Mbappé had struck 19 Champions League goals before he celebrated his 20th birthday. In comparison, Messi had two and Ronaldo hadn't scored at all. The fab Frenchman also raced to 100 goals for club and country much quicker. He was only 20 years and 173 days old when he hit a century of strikes. Ronaldo was almost 23 when he hit the same mark, while Messi was 22 years and 97 days.

Aged 20, Kylian had four league titles in his locker, while Messi had two and Cristiano, again, had zero. Plus, he had won the World Cup as a 19-year-old, which the other two had never done. With similar skills, speed and goal threats on the pitch, only time will tell if Mbappé goes on to have the greatest career of all three of these heroes!

CLASSY CHAMP

In 2020, plenty more awards and trophies were placed in Mbappé's bulging trophy cabinet!

More team and individual glory came Mbappé's way in 2019-20 as Paris Saint-Germain stormed to success. Despite the season ending early in March because of the Covid-19 outbreak, runaway leaders PSG were still crowned as champions. It was Kylian's fourth league trophy in a row.

FOOTY FACT

Of Mbappé's first 90 goals for PSG, he scored 70 with his right foot, 18 with his left and two headers.

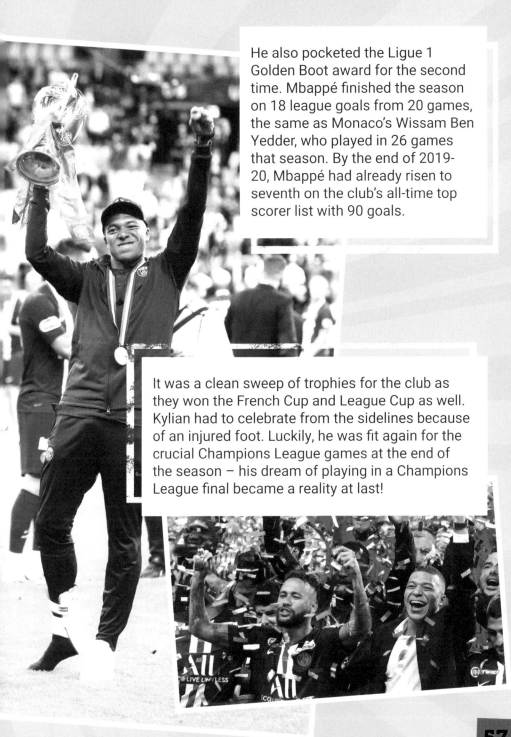

He also pocketed the Ligue 1 Golden Boot award for the second time. Mbappé finished the season on 18 league goals from 20 games, the same as Monaco's Wissam Ben Yedder, who played in 26 games that season. By the end of 2019-20, Mbappé had already risen to seventh on the club's all-time top scorer list with 90 goals.

It was a clean sweep of trophies for the club as they won the French Cup and League Cup as well. Kylian had to celebrate from the sidelines because of an injured foot. Luckily, he was fit again for the crucial Champions League games at the end of the season – his dream of playing in a Champions League final became a reality at last!

FINAL FIGHT

His first Champions League final appearance arrived after another impressive European season

PSG enjoyed their best ever season in the Champions League in 2019-20, with Mbappé one of their main men yet again. The French giants reached their first semi-final in 25 years, then made the final for the first time in their history!

FOOTY FACT

In the 2019-20 Champions League, Mbappé scored five goals from ten appearances and made five assists.

Kylian's European campaign kicked off with a 21-minute hat-trick during a 5-0 thrashing of Club Brugge. He scored in a dramatic 2-2 draw at Real Madrid as PSG topped their group in style. Another goal in a win against Galatasaray came before overcoming Borussia Dortmund in the first knockout round. He set up the winner against Atalanta in the quarter-final and helped run RB Leipzig ragged in the semi, which PSG won 3-0.

In the final, Mbappé's PSG faced a red-hot Bayern Munich team. Bayern narrowly beat them 1-0 with Mbappé's France teammate Kingsley Coman scoring the winner for the Germans. It was a big blow for the 21-year-old, who had battled to reward PSG with their first Champions League crown. It wasn't to be this year, but one day Europe's greatest club trophy will belong to him.

GREATEST GOALS

The striker has netted over 100 goals already, but these are the best of the best!

CLEVER CHIP

Opponent: Guingamp
Date: August 18 2018

On his PSG debut, he glided into the box and chipped the keeper with a cool right-foot finish.

SLICK SWITCH

Opponent: Russia
Date: March 27 2018

His second goal for France was a clever switch inside a defender before beating the keeper low at the near post.

LONG RANGER

Opponent: Lille
Date: November 2 2018

He loves to shoot from distance, and this bending beauty dipped perfectly into the net as Lille's defenders looked on in amazement!

FAB FLICK

Opponent: Nantes
Date: December 4 2019

Showing outrageous skill, Mbappé pounced on Angel Di Maria's cross to finish with a cheeky back heel that dazzled the keeper!

COOL CURL

Opponent: Borussia Dortmund
Date: April 12 2017

In a high pressure Champions League quarter-final, Kylian raced clear to curl a first-time effort around the goalkeeper to lead 3-1.

THE FUTURE OF FOOTBALL

Don't take your eyes off Kylian – he'll be bossing games and grabbing goals for years to come

He already has more trophies, awards and prizes than most players can even dream of, but Kylian Mbappé won't stop here. The striker powers on with his quest to become one of the all-time greats, fixing his place alongside the modern legends of Messi and Ronaldo and past heroes such as Pele, Maradona and Cryuff.

"I've learned a lot from all the successes and failures. My career will be built over the next 10 or 15 years." He's definitely a player to keep your eye on over the next decade, and could become one of the world's best ever players.

Having achieved so much at such a young age, Mbappé has set incredibly high standards. After ripping up Ligue 1 and Europe as an 18-year-old at Monaco, his big move to PSG didn't faze him. He seems to love smashing records, performing on the big stage and showing off his mix of speed, skill and deadly finishing. He has many years to wow the crowds, dazzle at tournaments and make his name as a formidable goalscorer. The France national team will always be a danger when he's on the pitch.

The fans take huge joy in watching him in action. He plays with a big smile, but make no mistake of the ruthless way he wants to win every game. Defenders must watch Mbappé very closely, and so should you!

CREDITS

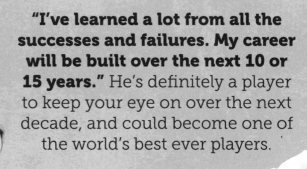

"I've learned a lot from all the successes and failures. My career will be built over the next 10 or 15 years." He's definitely a player to keep your eye on over the next decade, and could become one of the world's best ever players.

Having achieved so much at such a young age, Mbappé has set incredibly high standards. After ripping up Ligue 1 and Europe as an 18-year-old at Monaco, his big move to PSG didn't faze him. He seems to love smashing records, performing on the big stage and showing off his mix of speed, skill and deadly finishing. He has many years to wow the crowds, dazzle at tournaments and make his name as a formidable goalscorer. The France national team will always be a danger when he's on the pitch.

The fans take huge joy in watching him in action. He plays with a big smile, but make no mistake of the ruthless way he wants to win every game. Defenders must watch Mbappé very closely, and so should you!

CREDITS

Front Cover Lionel Urman/Abaca Press/Alamy Images
Back Cover Julien Poupart/Abaca Press/Alamy Images; Stephane Mahe/Reuters/Alamy Images
Graphics - Irina Qiwi/Shutterstock
6-7 Xavier Laine/Contributor - Getty Images Sport/Getty Images; Scoop Dyga/Contributor – Icon Sport/Getty Images; Tim Clayton - Corbis/Contributor - Corbis Sport/Getty Images
8-9 Baptiste Fernandez/Contributor – Icon Sport/Getty Images
10-11 Pictures: Stephane Cardinale - Corbis/Contributor - Corbis Sport/Getty Images; Jean Catuffe/Contributor - Getty Images Sport/Getty Images **Words:** wikipedia.org
12-13 Jean Catuffe/Contributor – Getty Images Sport/Getty Images; Dave Winter/Contributor - Icon Sport/Getty Images, Icon Sport/Contributor - Icon Sport/Getty Images; FRANCK FIFE/Contributor - AFP/Getty Images
14-15 FRANCK FIFE/Staff – AFP/Getty Images; Srdjan Stevanovic/Contributor – Getty Images Sport/Getty Images
16-17 Laurence Griffiths/Staff – Getty Images Sport/Getty Images; ullstein bild/Contributor – ullstein bild/Getty Images; Pool MERILLON/STEVENS/Contributor – Gamma-Rapho/Getty Images; Clive Mason/Staff – Getty Images Sport/Getty Images; CHRISTOPHE SIMON/Contributor – AFP/Getty Images
18-19 AFP Contributor/Contributor - AFP/Getty Images; VI Images/Contributor - Getty Images Sport/Getty Images
20-21 Pictures: Stu Forster/Staff – Getty Images Sport/Getty Images; Jean Catuffe/Contributor – Getty Images Sport/Getty Images **Words:** Sam Pilger: bleacherreport.com
22-23 Pictures: Ian Watson/Staff - Getty Images Sport Classic/Getty Images; Dave Winter/Contributor – Icon Sport/Getty Images **Words:** Sam Maguire: footballwhispers.com
24-25 Dave Winter/Contributor – Icon Sport/Getty Images; Xavier Laine/Contributor – Getty Images Sport/Getty Images
26-27 Pictures: Alexander Scheuber/Stringer – Bongarts/Getty Images; Ronald Wittek/Stringer – Bongarts/Getty Images **Words:** UEFA.com
28-29 BORIS HORVAT/Staff - AFP/Getty Images
30-31 Dave Winter/Contributor - Icon Sport/Getty Images; OLI SCARFF/Stringer – AFP/Getty Images; UEFA/Handout - Getty Images Sport/Getty Images
32-33 Pictures: Aurelien Meunier/Stringer - Getty Images Sport/Getty Images; Anthony Dibon/Contributor – Icon Sport/Getty Images **Words:** Jonathan Johnson: espn.co.uk
34-35 Xavier Laine/Contributor – Getty Images Sport/Getty Image
36-37 Pictures: Dave Winter/Contributor – Icon Sport/Getty Images; Frederic Stevens/Contributor - Getty Images Sport/Getty Images; Shaun Botterill/Contributor - FIFA/Getty Images; Catherine Steenkeste/Contributor - Getty Images Sport/Getty Images; SOPA Images - Contributor/LightRocket/Getty Images **Words:** FIFA.com, Joe Wright: goal.com, PSG.fr
38-39 Pictures: Kyodo News/Contributor - Kyodo News/Getty Images; FRANCK FIFE/Contributor – AFP/Getty Images; Jean Catuffe/Contributor – Getty Images Sport/Getty Images; Dave Winter/Contributor – Icon Sport/Getty Images; Laurence Griffiths/Staff - Getty Images Sport/Getty Images **Words:** FIFA.com, Tom Sunderland: bleacherreport.com, Glenn Price: espn.co.uk
40-41 Soccrates Images/Contributor - Getty Images Sport/Getty Images; Jean Catuffe/Contributor - Getty Images Sport/Getty Images; FRANCK FIFE/Contributor – AFP/Getty Images
42-43 Frederic Stevens/Contributor - Getty Images Sport/Getty Images; Dave Winter/Contributor - Icon Sport/Getty Images
44-45 Anthony Dibon/Contributor – Icon Sport/Getty Images; TF-Images/Contributor - Getty Images Sport/Getty Images; China News Service/Contributor - China News Service/Getty Images
46-47 Pictures: Simon Stacpoole/Offside/Contributor – Offside/Getty Images; Chris Brunskill/Fantasista/Contributor - Getty Images Sport/Getty Images; NurPhoto/Contributor – NurPhoto/Getty Images **Words:** FIFA.com
48-49 Pictures: Aurelien Meunier – Contributor – Getty Images Sport/Getty Images; Catherine Steenkeste/Contributor - Getty Images Sport/Getty Images; Jean Catuffe/Contributor - Getty Images Sport/Getty Images **Words:** Gregg Davies: fourfourtwo.com
50-51 Paris Saint-Germain Football/Contributor – PSG/Getty Images; Kirsty Sparrow/Contributor – Getty Images Entertainment/Getty Images; Frederic Stevens/Contributor – Getty Images Sport/Getty Images; Aurelien Meunier/Contributor - PSG/Getty Images
52-53 Anthony Dibon/Contributor – Icon Sport/Getty Images; Scoop Dyga/Contributor - Icon Sport/Getty Images; Aurelien Meunier/Contributor - PSG/Getty Images
54-55 MARTIN BUREAU/Contributor – AFP/Getty Images; Michael Regan/Staff - Getty Images Sport/Getty Images; Jonathan Moscrop/Contributor - Getty Images Sport/Getty Images
56-57 Vincent Michel/Contributor - Icon Sport/Getty Images; Scoop Dyga/Contributor – Icon Sport/Getty Images; Jean Catuffe/Contributor - Getty Images Sport/Getty Images
58-59 David Ramos/Staff – Getty Images Sport/Getty Images; Pool/Pool - Getty Images Sport/Getty Images; DAVID RAMOS/Contributor – AFP/Getty Images
60-61 Baptiste Fernandez/Contributor – Icon Sport/Getty Images; FRANCK FIFE/Contributor – AFP/Getty Images; Catherine Steenkeste/Contributor - Getty Images Sport/Getty Images; Xavier Laine/Contributor – Getty Images Sport/Getty Images; Maja Hitij/Staff - Bongarts/Getty Images
62-63 Pictures: Marc Atkins/Contributor - Getty Images Sport/Getty Image **Words:** FIFA.com